Fly High with Lawnchair Larry

Marcy Schaaf

Dear Dreamer,

Have you ever looked up at the sky and wondered what it would feel like to fly? Have you ever had a big dream that seemed a little too wild or impossible? Well, this is the true story of a man named Larry Walters, who dreamed the most extraordinary dream—and made it come true with a little courage, a lot of creativity, and a lawn chair!

Larry didn't let fear or doubt stop him. He took something as simple as balloons and a chair and turned them into a soaring adventure. His story is a reminder that no dream is too big if you believe in yourself and take that first brave step.

This book is for all the kids who dare to dream, who want to reach for the stars (or the clouds), and who know deep down that the only limits are the ones we place on ourselves.

So, let's take a seat in Larry's chair and discover how one man's dream lifted him higher than he ever imagined. And remember: you don't need wings to fly—you just need a dream and the courage to follow it!

Keep dreaming big,

Author

Marcy Schaaf

Larry Walters had a dream, oh
so grand,
To rise up high, above the land.

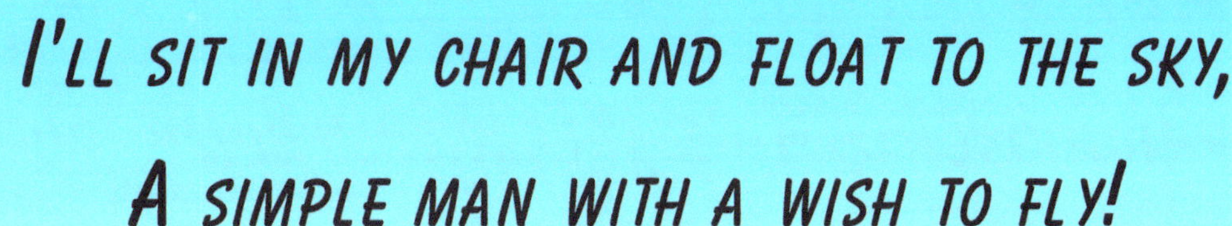

I'll sit in my chair and float to the sky,
A simple man with a wish to fly!

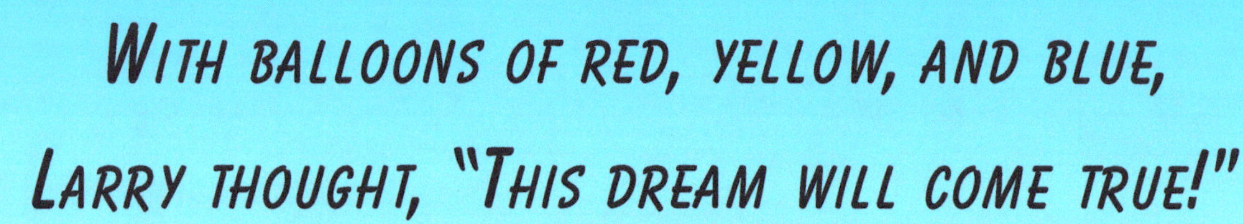

With balloons of red, yellow, and blue,
Larry thought, "This dream will come true!"

He tied them tight, with knots so neat,
Then grabbed a soda and a snack to eat.

Up, up he went, into the air,
Larry, the man with the flying chair!

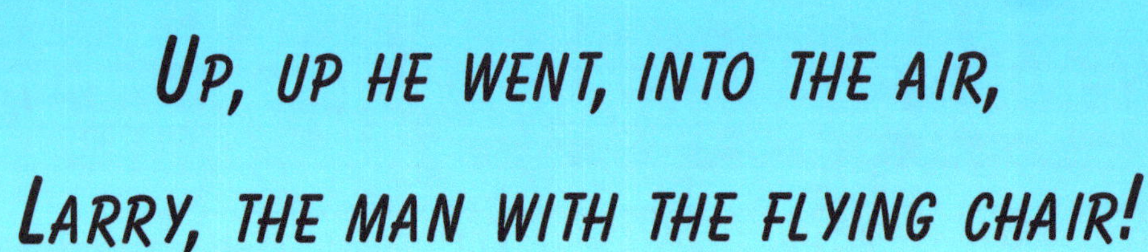

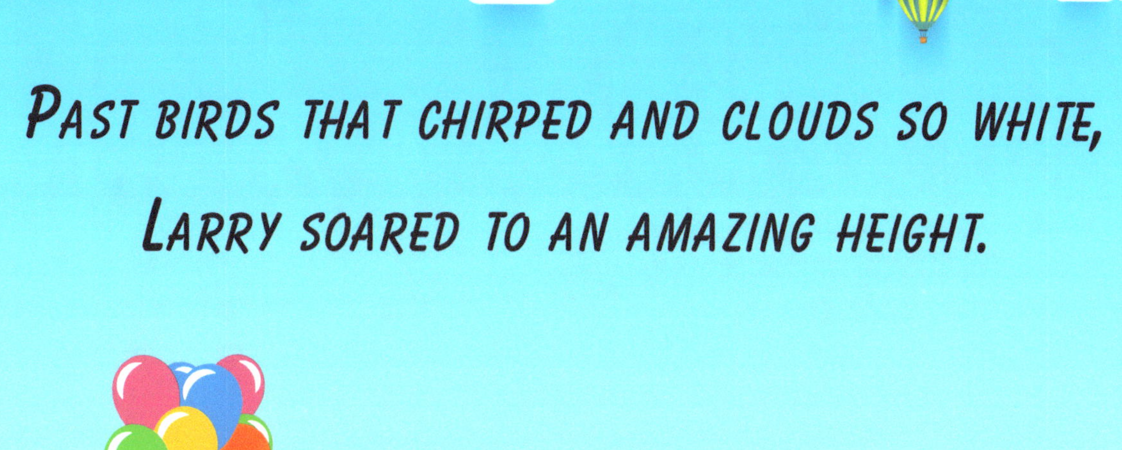

Past birds that chirped and clouds so white,
Larry soared to an amazing height.

But oh, dear me, what a surprise!
He floated too far, way up in the skies.

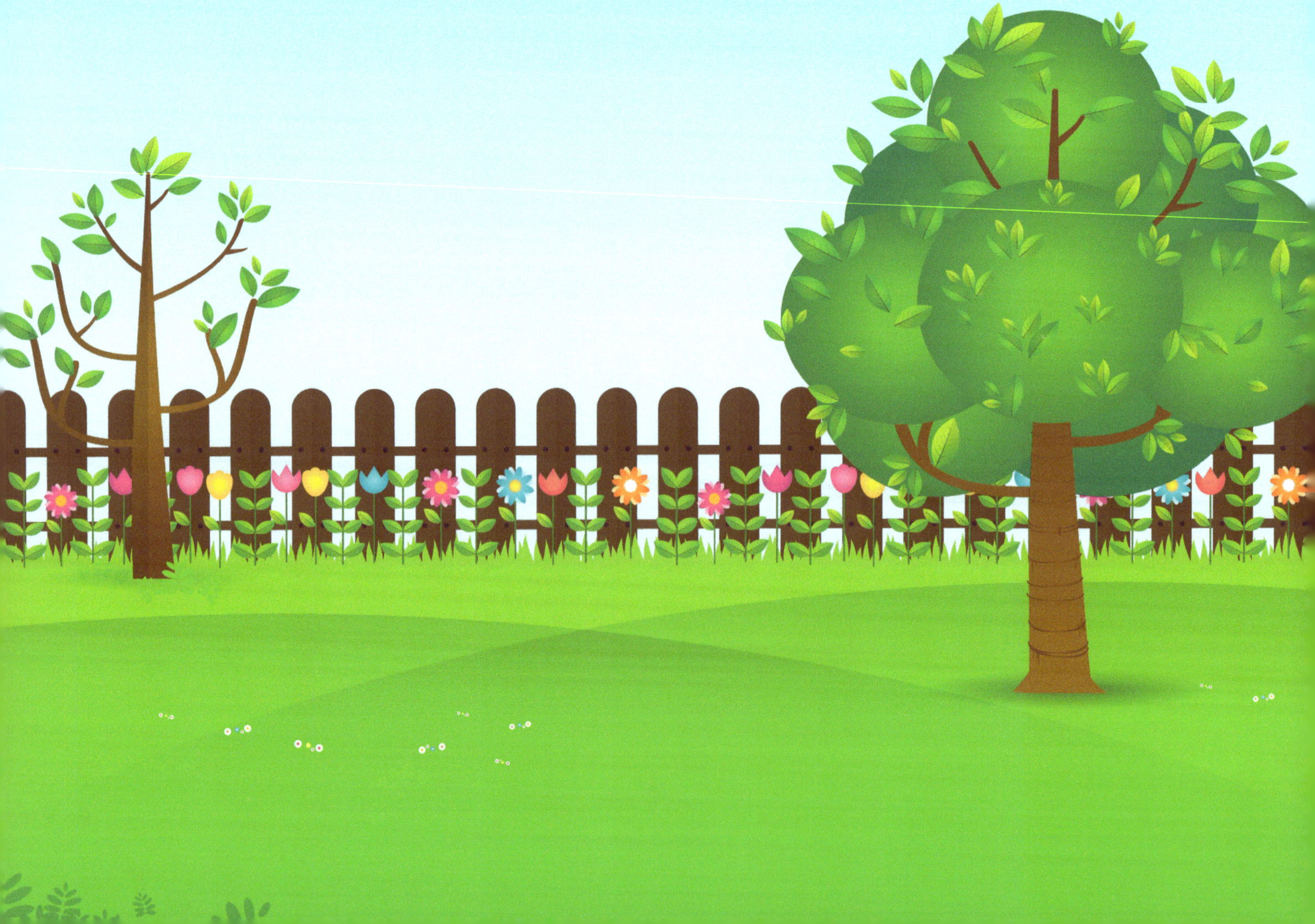

At sixteen thousand feet he sat
Waving hello to a passing cat.

PLANES FLEW BY WITH PILOTS WHO STARED,

AT LARRY'S BALLOONS AND THE CHAIR HE DARED.

"I'll pop some balloons, and down I'll go,"
Said Larry with a confident glow.

Bang! Bang! The balloons went "pop!"
Slowly, Larry began to drop.

DOWN THROUGH THE CLOUDS, HE MADE HIS WAY,
BACK TO THE GROUND AT THE END OF THE DAY.

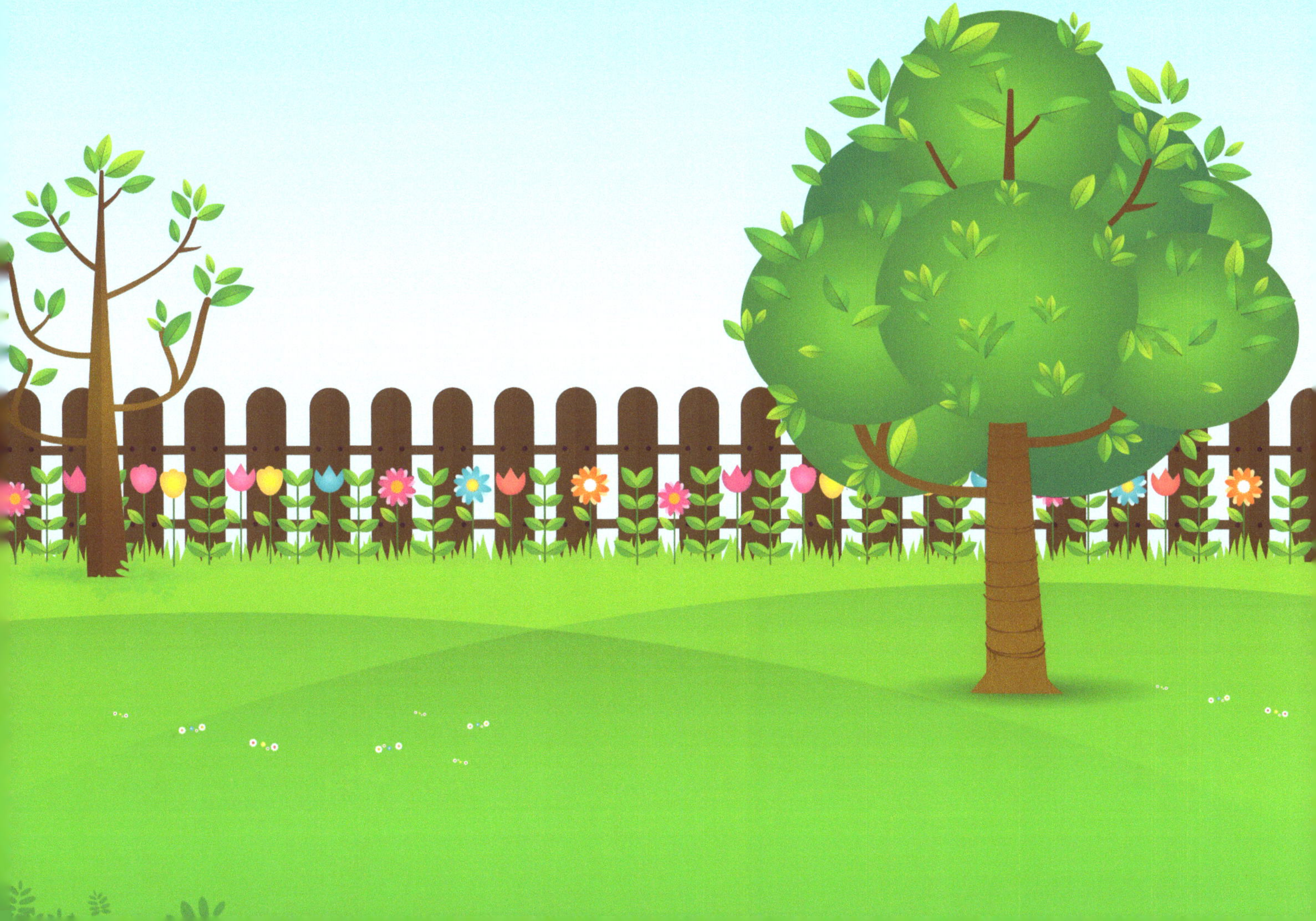

NEIGHBORS GATHERED, POINTING IN AWE,
AT THE MAN WHO FLEW WITH NO FLAW.

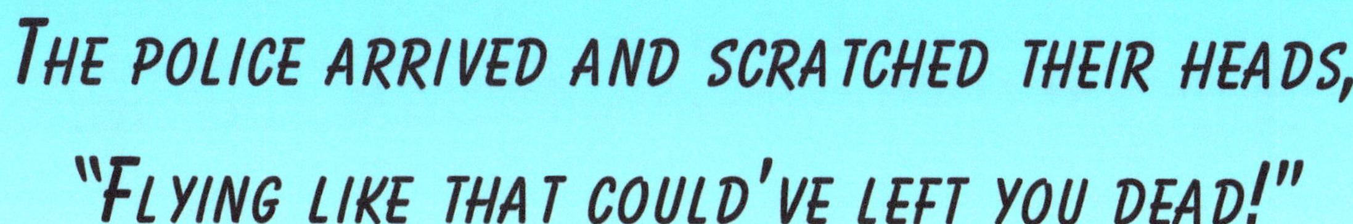

The police arrived and scratched their heads,
"Flying like that could've left you dead!"

Larry just smiled and said with a cheer,
"I wanted to fly—I had no fear!"

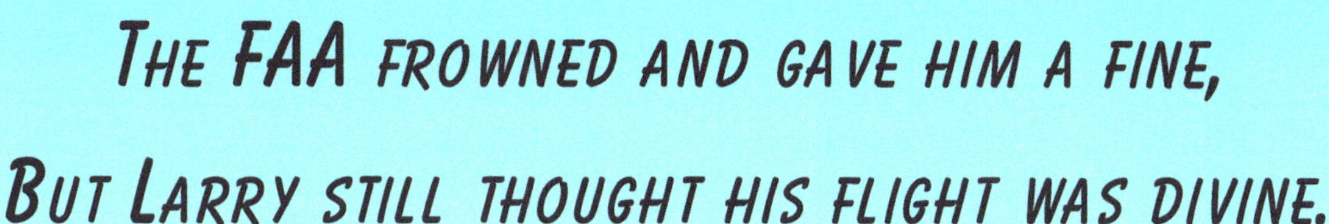

The FAA frowned and gave him a fine,
But Larry still thought his flight was divine.

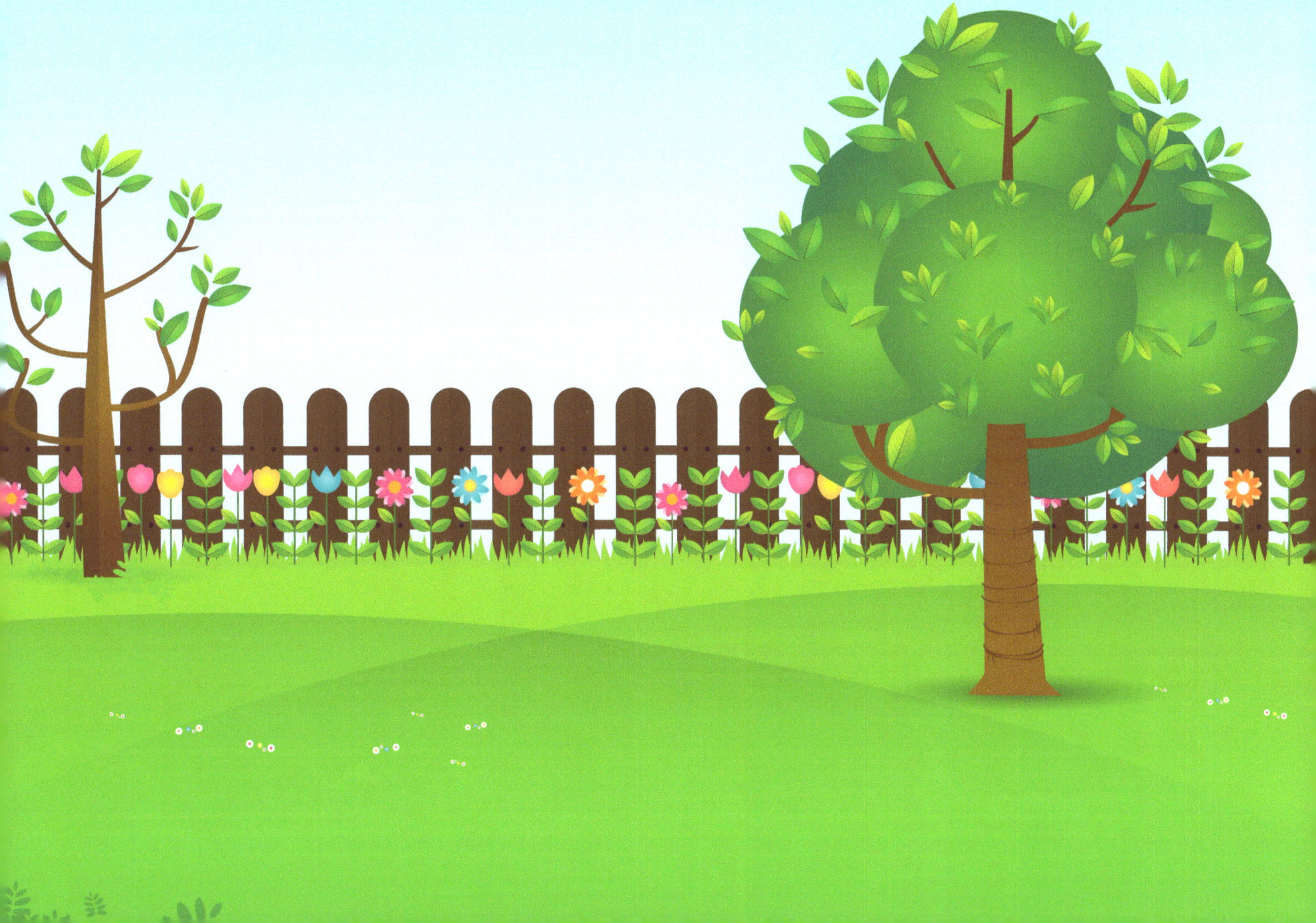

A hero he became in papers and news,
For chasing a dream in red, yellow, and blue hues.

Kids cheered,

"We love Larry, the flying man!"

He inspired them to dream and plan.

Larry said, "Dream big, my friends so dear,
But be prepared and have no fear!"

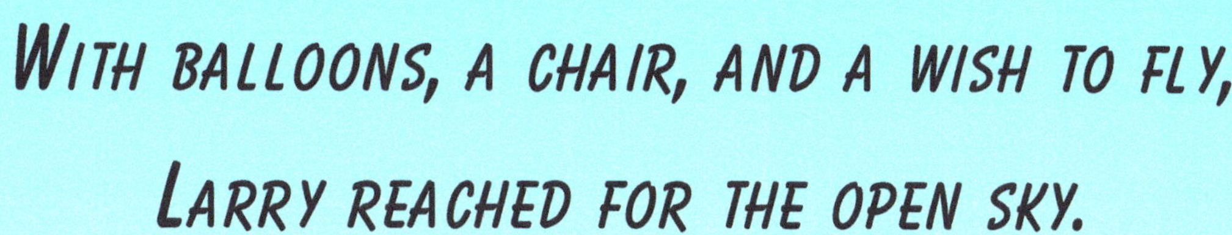

With balloons, a chair, and a wish to fly,
Larry reached for the open sky.

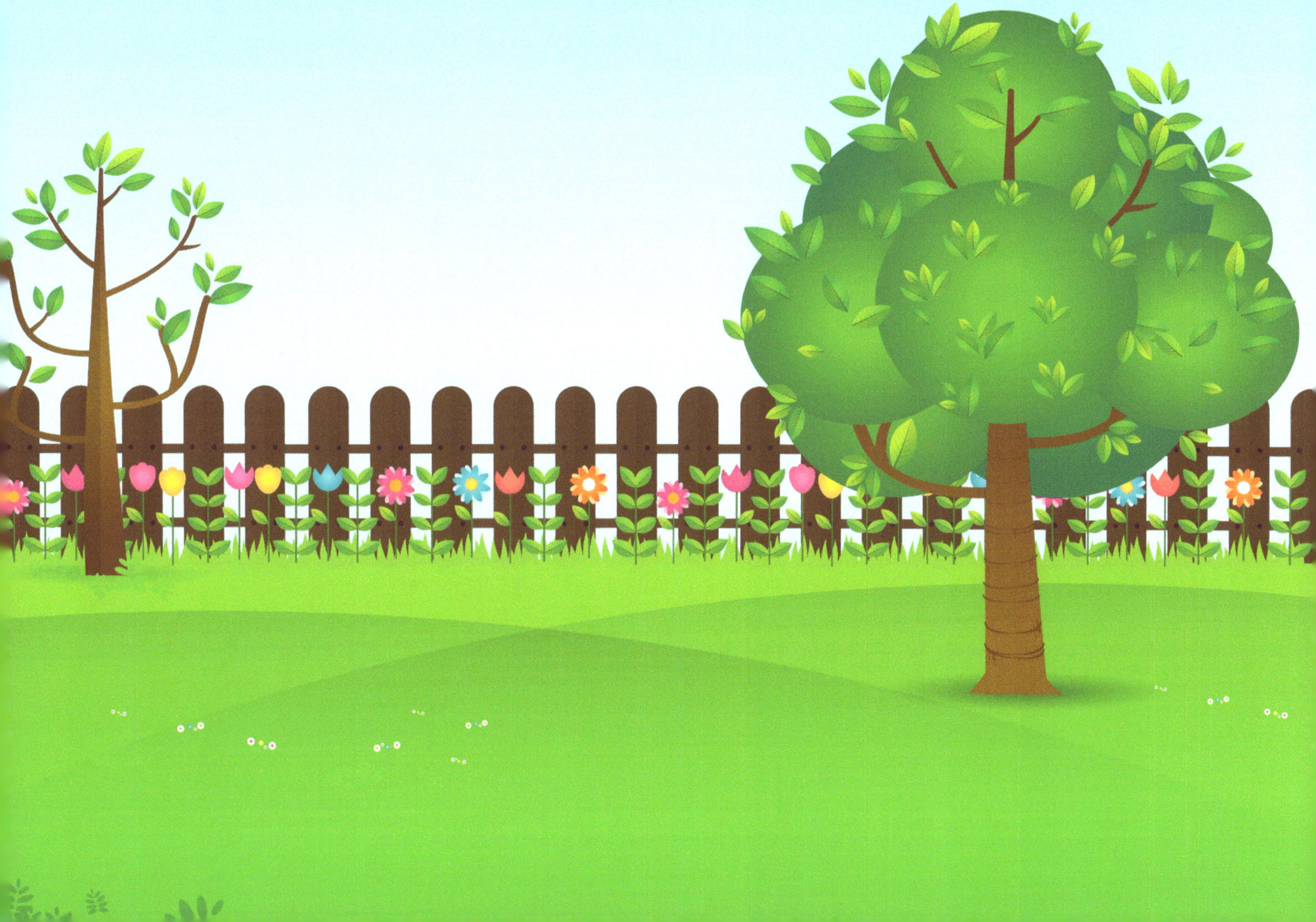

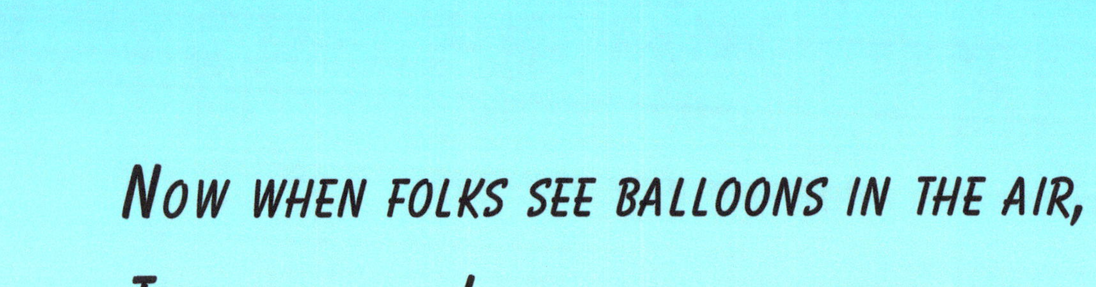

Now when folks see balloons in the air,
They think of Larry and his brave flair.

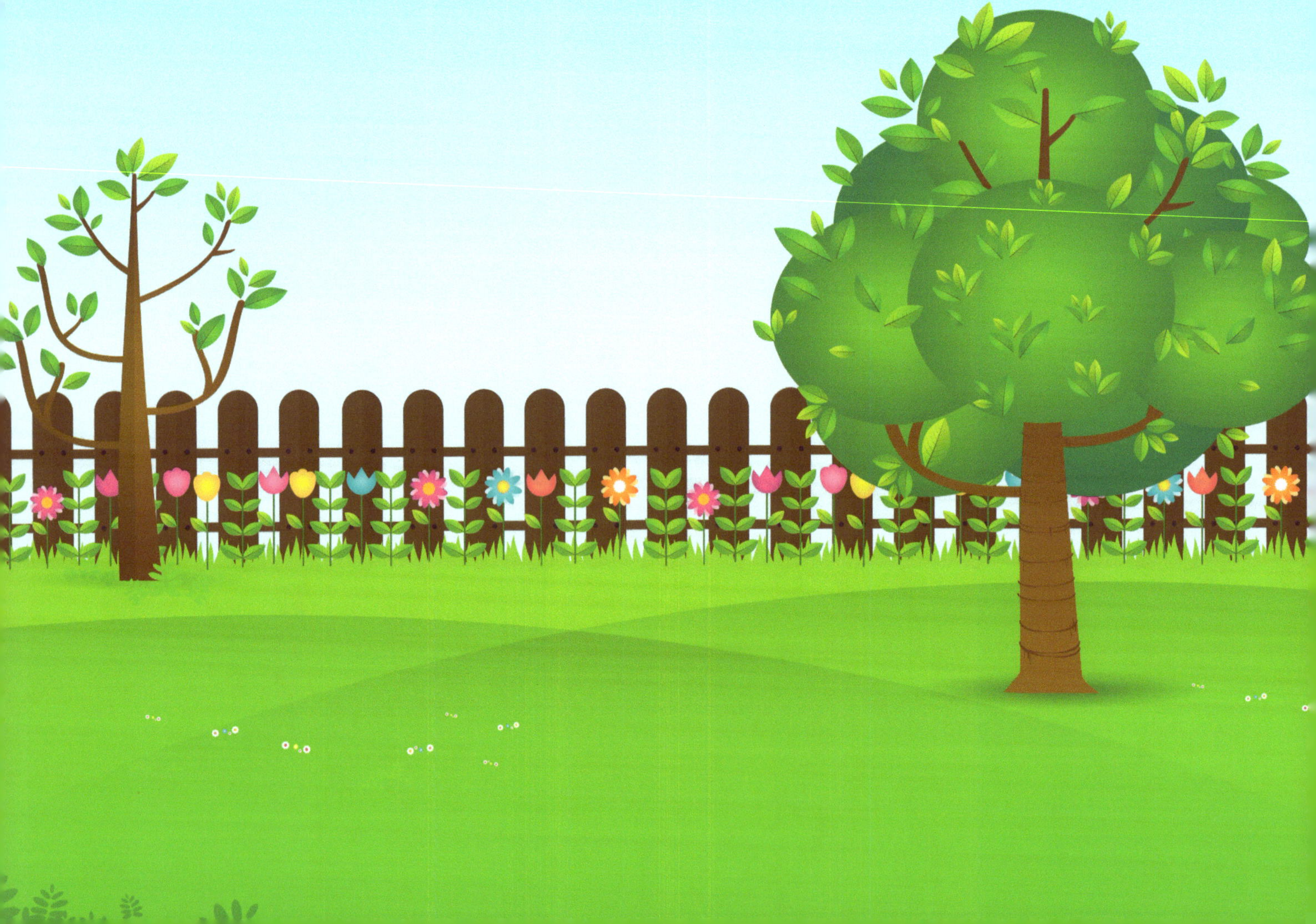

So remember Larry and what he'd say,
"A man can't just sit all day!"

He proved that dreams can lift us high,
Even if we're just an ordinary guy.

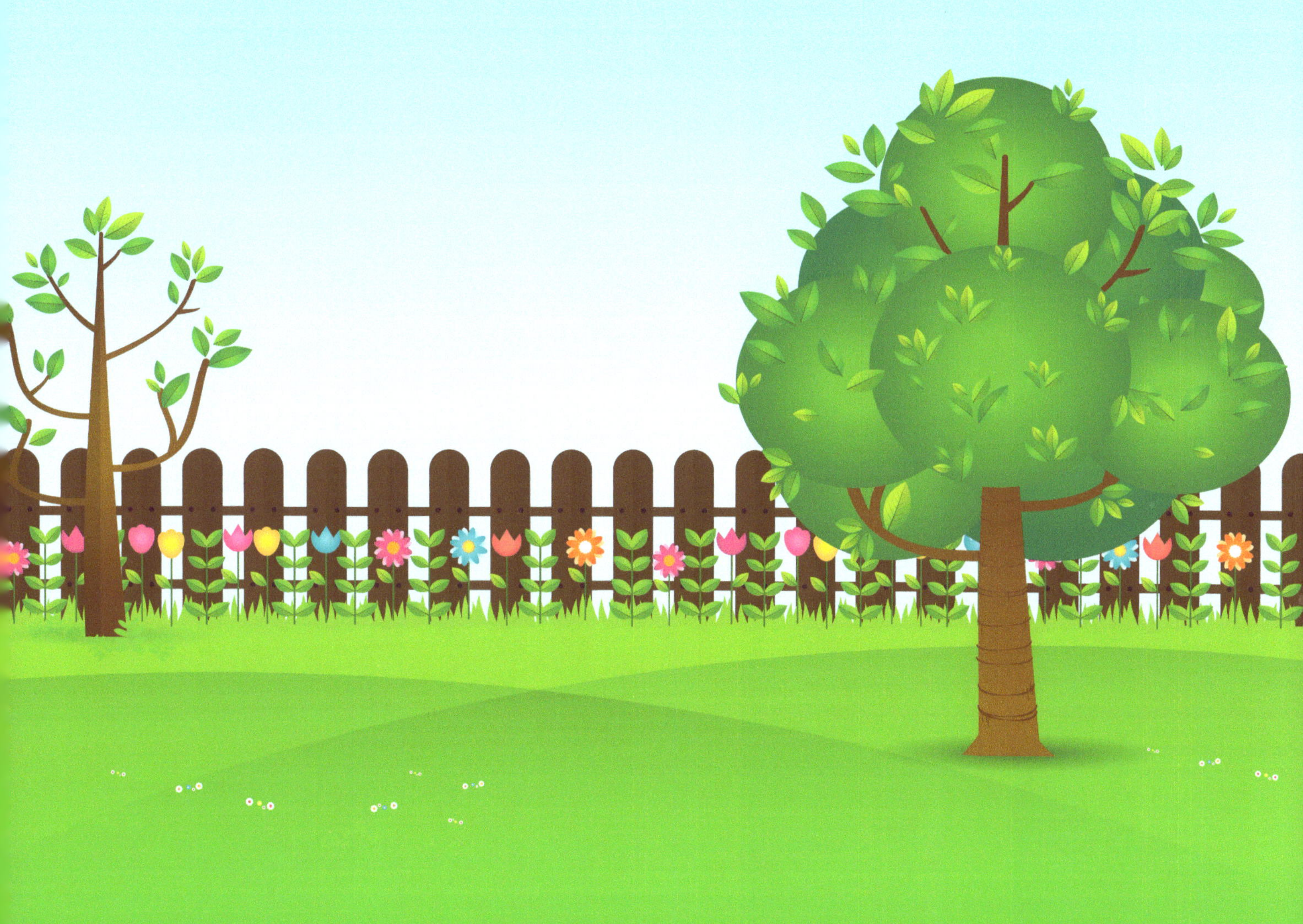

His story's told in books and song,
Larry's adventure will last so long.

If ever you feel your dream's too high,
Think of Larry and give it a try.

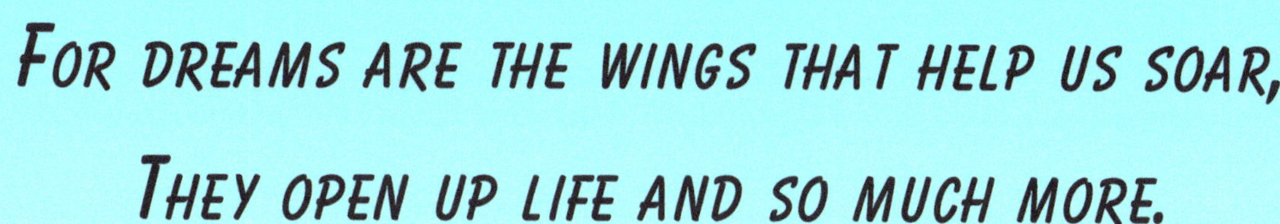
For dreams are the wings that help us soar,
They open up life and so much more.

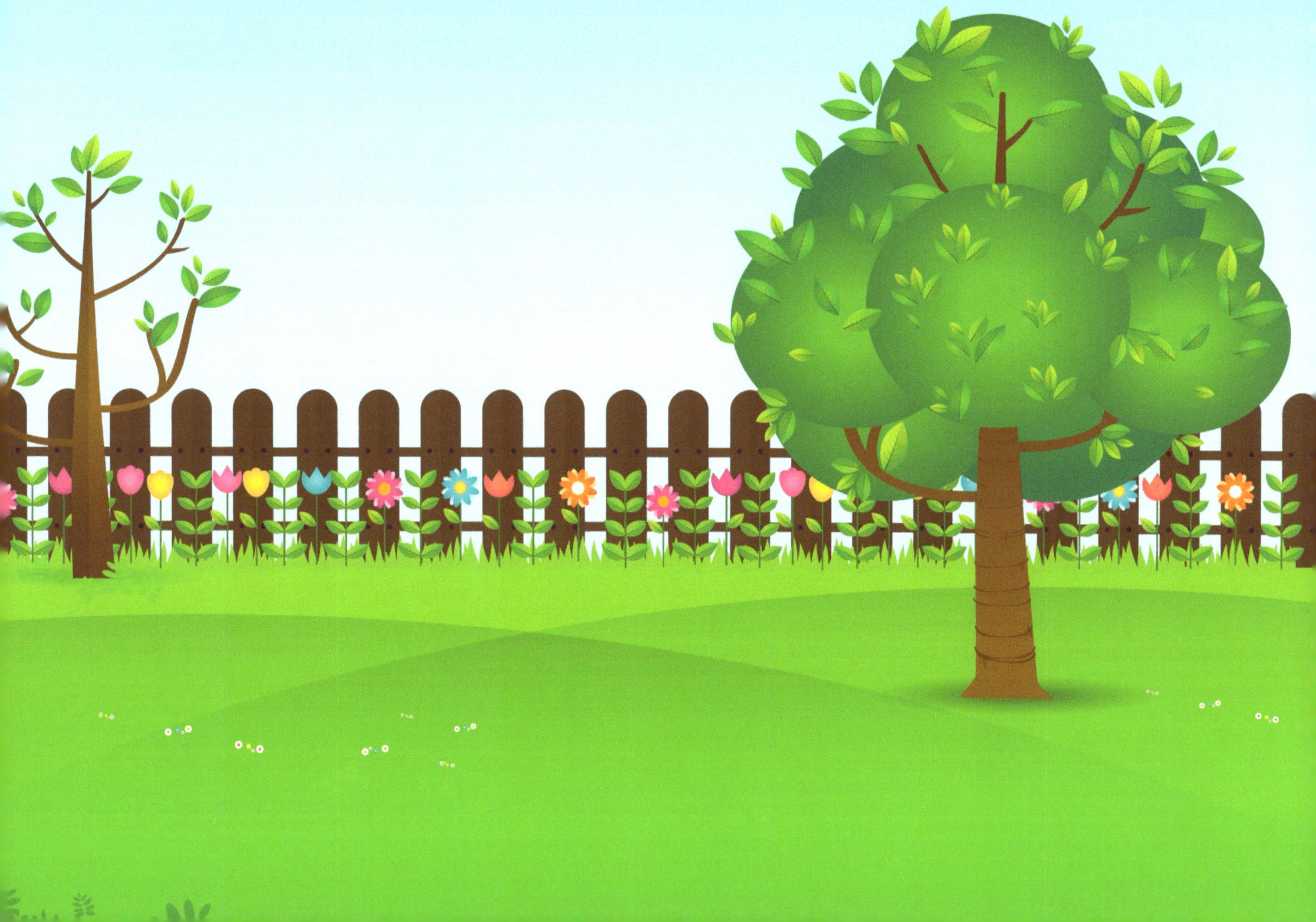

Be bold, be brave, take a chance,
And maybe one day, you'll dance!

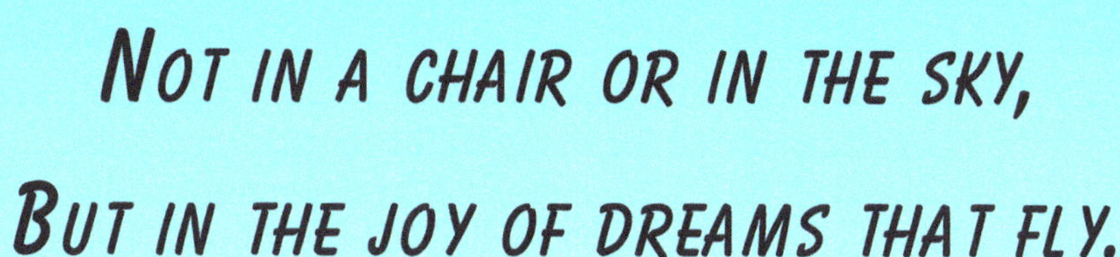

Not in a chair or in the sky,
But in the joy of dreams that fly.

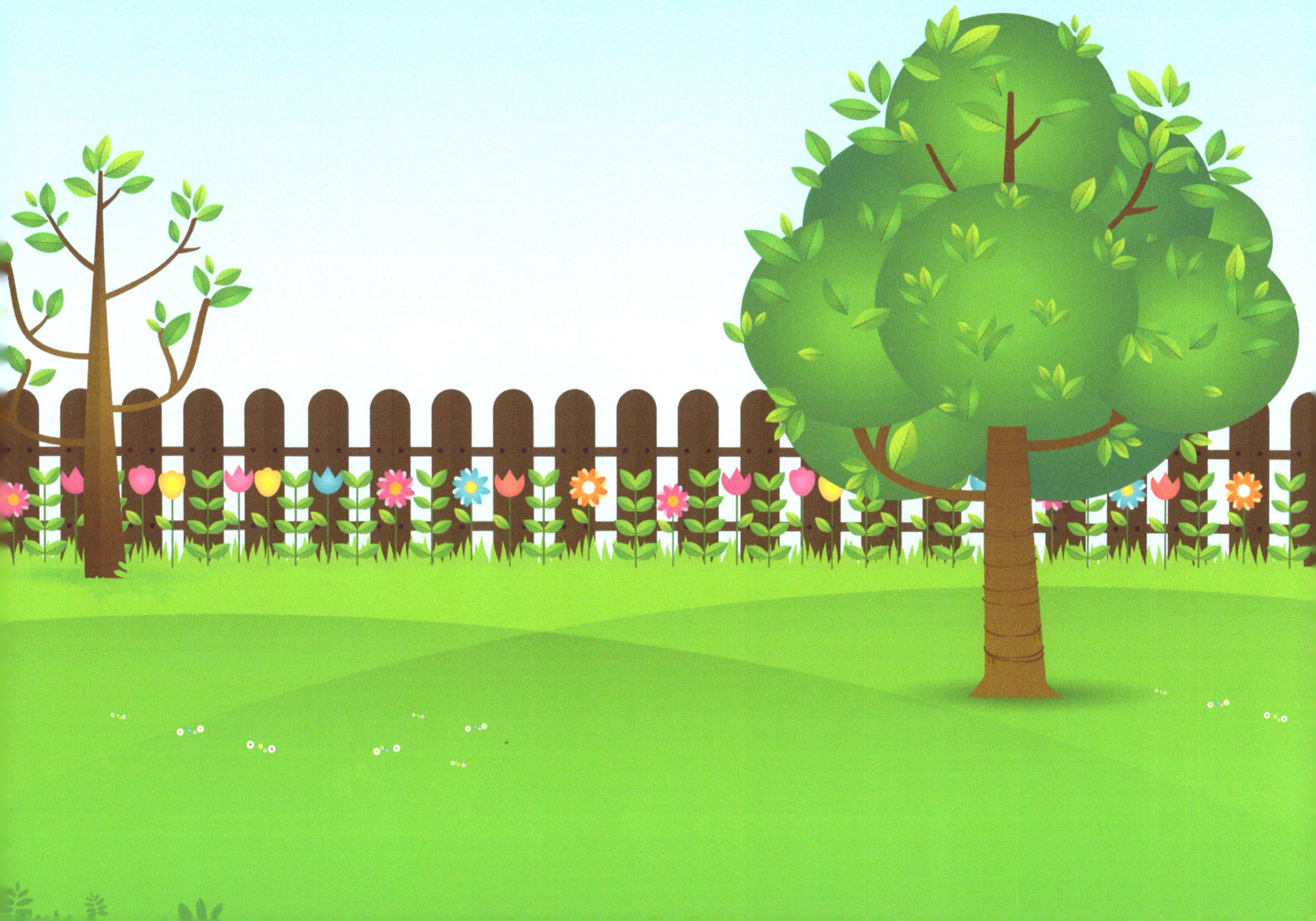

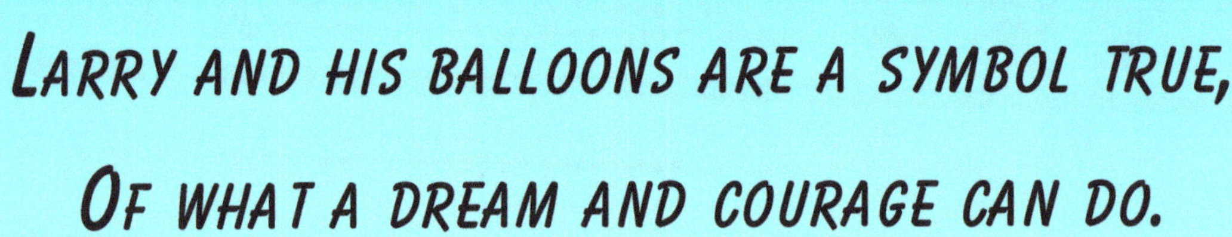

LARRY AND HIS BALLOONS ARE A SYMBOL TRUE,
OF WHAT A DREAM AND COURAGE CAN DO.

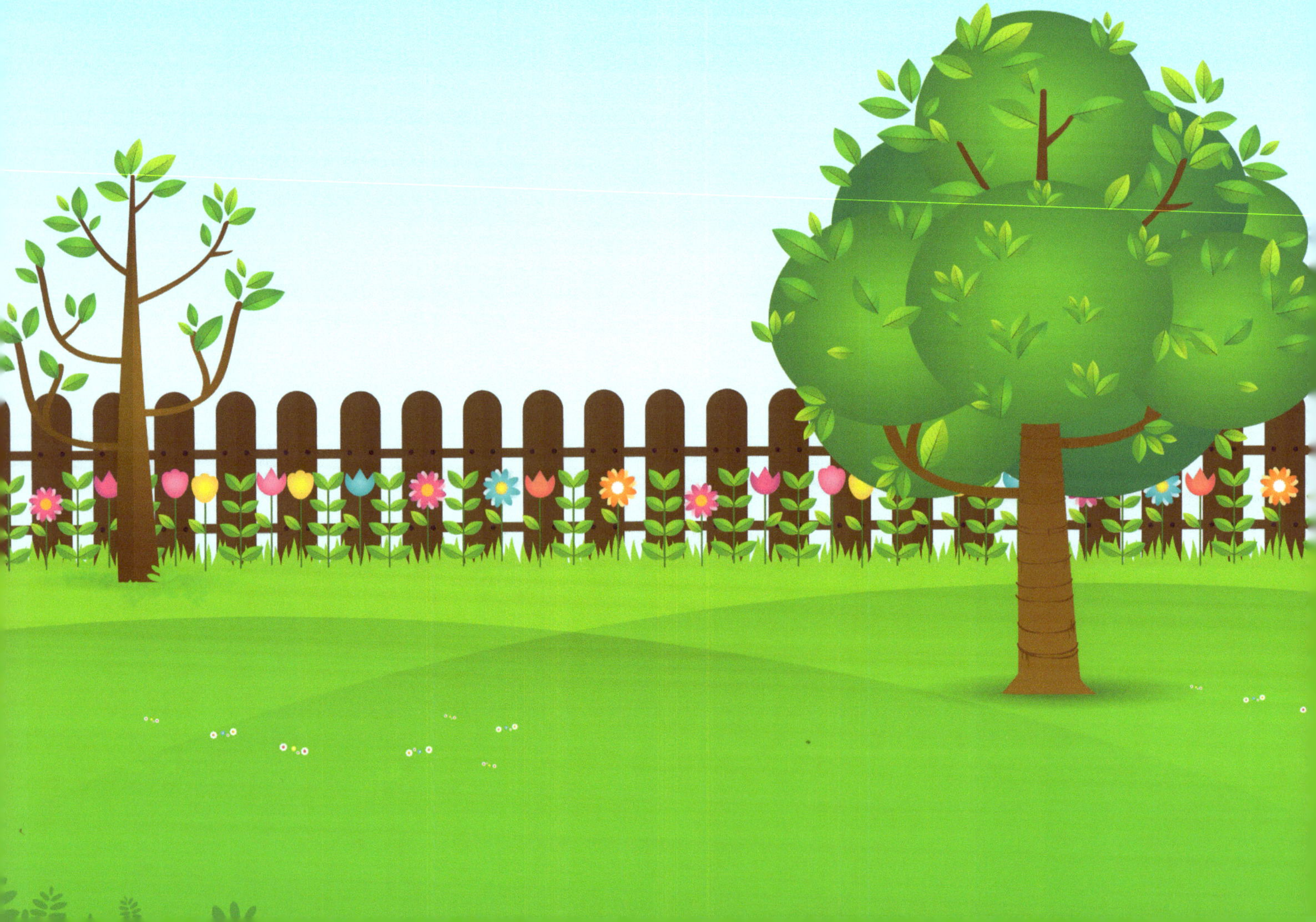

So tie your dreams to your heart with care,
And like Larry, fly anywhere!

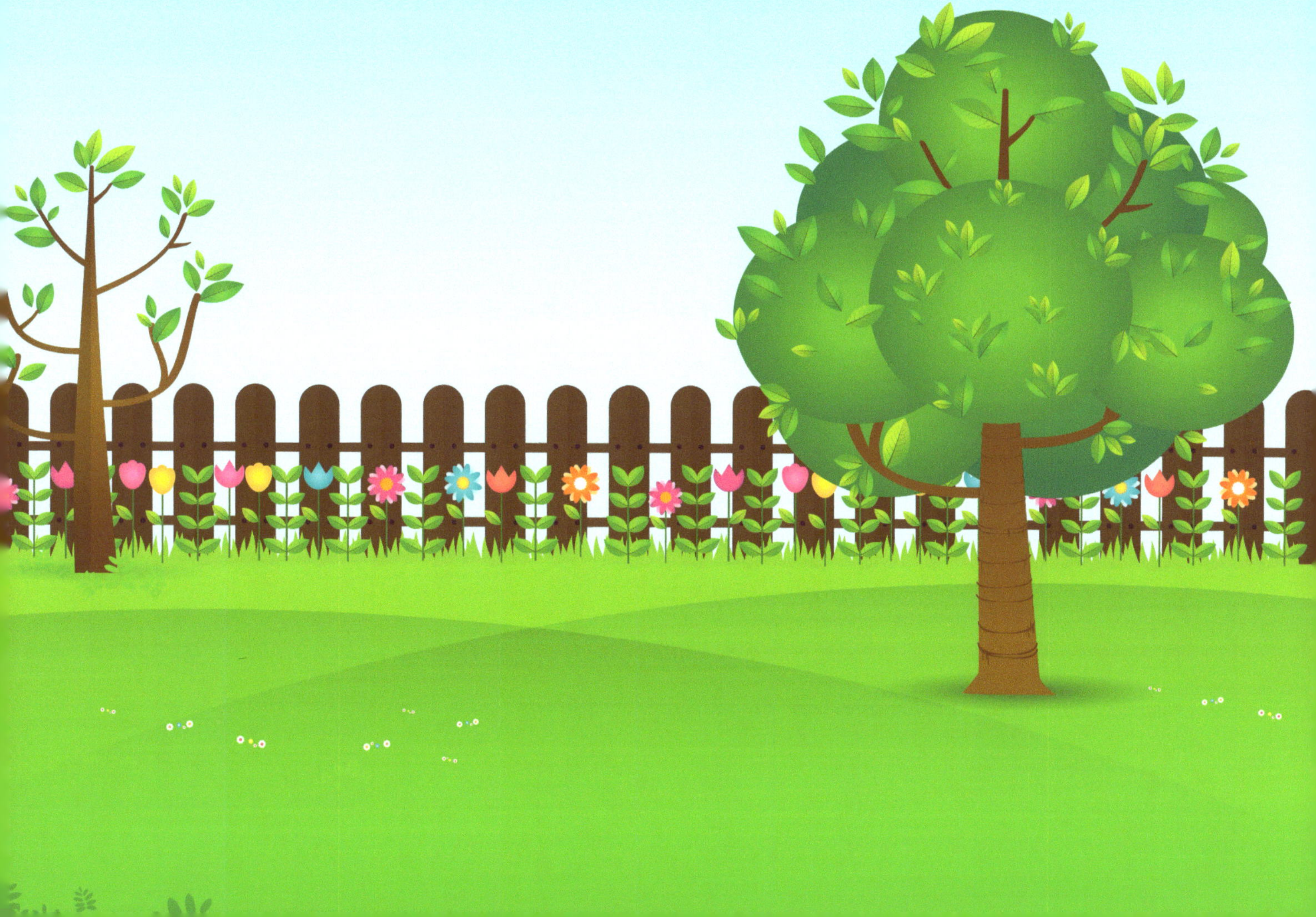

Larry Walters, famously known as "Lawnchair Larry," has inspired various creative works across different media. Here are some notable examples:

Books:

"The Man in the Flying Lawn Chair" by George Plimpton: This profile, published in The New Yorker in 1998, delves into Larry Walters' unique flight and its implications.

The New Yorker

"Larry Walters: The Witty Story Of A Lawnchair Flight And Its Pilot" by John Stewart: This book offers an in-depth look at Larry's remarkable life and his daring adventure.

Magers & Quinn Booksellers

Songs:

"Larry Walters (Lawnchair Larry)" by Michael Hearst: Featured on the album Songs For Extraordinary People, this track narrates Larry's adventurous flight.

Spotify

"Larry Walters" by Miscellaneous Owl: This song reflects on Larry's journey, capturing the whimsical nature of his flight.

Miscellaneous Owl

"Lawn Chair Larry" from the musical 42 Balloons: This song is part of a musical that centers on Larry Walters' flight, highlighting his daring spirit.

Playbill

Poems:

While there may not be widely recognized poems solely dedicated to Larry Walters, his story has inspired various creative expressions, including songs and articles, that capture the poetic essence of his adventure.

These works showcase the enduring fascination with Lawnchair Larry's unique and daring flight, reflecting his impact on popular culture.

Join Our Book of the Month Club!

Looking for the perfect gift that keeps on giving? Join our Book of the Month Club! For just $25 a month, or $250 if you purchase a year upfront, you or your loved ones will receive a handpicked children's book every month, straight to your doorstep.

Here's how it works:
Choose from 15 different languages to receive bilingual books that make learning fun.
Enjoy monthly shipments of our exclusive books that inspire, teach, and entertain children of all ages.
Each month's book is carefully selected to provide a new adventure, valuable lesson, and a chance to explore cultures from around the world.
It's the perfect gift for birthdays, holidays, or just because! Whether you're nurturing a young reader or encouraging language learning, our Book of the Month Club is designed to bring joy to every bookshelf.

Exclusive Bonus: As part of your membership, you'll also receive a monthly podcast about our featured book delivered straight to your email! Listen in for behind-the-scenes insights, fun facts, and tips for making storytime even more magical.

Sign up today at www.Booksbyschaaf.com and start enjoying the gift of reading all year long!

Books By Schaaf

www.BookBySchaaf.com

Podcast series about our book on TikTok.

Activity Guide companion's for each storybook can be found on our website.

Find us at: